UNDERSTANDING THE PROCESS
"THE ITES"

I0173298

An in depth discussion on how you can be victorious in prayer by "understanding the process;" what happens when you pray. Learn key elements of whom and the enemy is.

BY
ALVIN L. ARMSTRONG

Published by Stewart Publishing
And
Alvin Armstrong Ministries

Understanding the Process
Copyright © 2008
Alvin L. Armstrong

ALL RIGHTS RESERVED

Unless otherwise indicated, all Scripture quotations are taken from the King James Version copyright © 1989 by World Publishing; Old Scofield Study System copyright © 1990, 1917 by Oxford University Press Inc.; Amplified Bible copyright © 1954, 1958, 1962 1964 by Lockman Foundation.

ISBN 978-0-615-22211-0
First printing: July 2008-200 copies

Additional copies of this book are available by mail.
Send $15.00 (includes tax and postage) to:
Alvin L. Armstrong Ministries
1003 Roleen Drive
Vallejo, CA 94589
707-643-0820

Please visit us at

Printed in the USA
by Morris Publishing
3212 East Highway 30
Kearney, NE 68847
800-650-7888

Dedication

This book is dedicated to my mom and dad, Solomon L. and Lourina Armstrong who tirelessly, took our family to church and taught us the Word of God at an early age. Their way of living was an example for us and we saw at an early age how to live for God at home and at Church.

Thank you both......

TABLE OF CONTENTS

Foreword

I am honored to write the foreword for my husband. There are many other people he could have asked. I thank him in advance for giving me the opportunity to introduce him to the world through this book. I met him over thirty years ago at his grandmother's home. Of course, we shared no mutual interest in each other. He was a "yucky" boy and I was a "yucky" girl.

God knew who I would need in my life, as well as whom my husband would need in his. As time passed we took an interest in one another and 33 years later here we are happily married and blessed to have 4 children and 6 grandchildren!

I consider myself a blessed woman to have such a mighty man of God in my life. He is a wonderful person. I am truly proud of all that he does. He is a husband, father, pastor, and provider. Yet he still finds time to be my friend and lover.

We are both in love with God. He is the foundation of our lives. During our ups and downs the key has been to first seek God and His Word for the answers to all that we go through in this life, and continue to do so. This book explains how you can be victorious every time you are in a hard place and what the "wilderness" represents and how too "GO THROUGHT IT", and not camp out in it.

Alvin has spent many hours fasting and praying to make sure the Word of God that was imparted to him is revealed to all who read this book, that it should be a blessing to you and that every need you have is met. You have not picked up this book by mistake. The Lord has a word for you today. It's your time to receive from the Lord. I pray that after reading this book you will have a better understanding of the process.

Sincerely, Lorraine Armstrong

Acknowledgements

This book was of course inspired by God to help others in the body of Christ to gain more revelation from God's Word. Except for the encouragement and support of friends and loved ones around me, at first it was hard for me to get around writing this book. So, I thank the following people for their invaluable assistance:

- To my wife, Lorraine who has stood by my side through thick and thin, you remain a great inspiration to me. To our children Dennielle, Montrell, Tamra, and Ramel: for their love and support and patience during my growth and maturity in the Lord and his Word.

- To my family at Church of the Redeemed, for their love and for encouragement me too write what God has given me.

- To my Pastor Dr, Philip G. Goudeaux, of Calvary Christian Center in Sacramento, CA for teaching me that I am somebody in Christ Jesus and to step out and be bold.

- To Cynthia Stewart, for her encouragement and for handling the publishing and editing process of this book.

INTRODUCTION

Have you ever had questions that never seem to get answered? Have you wondered why things are the way they are, or why is it so hard to live the life of a Christian? You know, we live our lives on this earth, and tests, trials, and temptations come, so you pray, you fast, and read God's Word but it doesn't seem to get better; your situation gets worse and it looks as if you are going downhill fast without any way to stop. Why does the pressure increase?

Question: Is God tempting and testing me to see if I can take it or handle things? Am I to just keep a stiff upper lip and stay stuck with whatever comes my way and accept it as God's will for my life?

These and other questions people *(as well as I)* have had and I knew some basic answers to them. But one day while I was in prayer, just fellowshipping with God, I picked up my Bible and began to read in the book of Exodus, chapter 23, and I was shocked and excited at the same time to see that God had answered all of my questions in a few verses. So now, let's begin our journey in this book to see and receive revelation knowledge of God's Word for our life.

Chapter
1

THE PROCESS BEGINS

Obeying Gods Voice – Part 1

God has spoken to us from His Word in Exodus, Chapter 23. He has answered the questions that we've had in our lives.

As a Pastor, I want to say this to you (the reader): I cannot speak on the things that you may want to hear. You have to be able to take what you need from the message in this book even if it hurts. It's hard to hear that we may be wrong about somethings, especially if you've attained a certain amount of success, but we have to accept it in order to change, in order to improve. It amazes me how we want the answers to our problems and we want things done, but when it comes to change and being constant, we fall off; however, when we experience something new or different, we are consistent in that "new" thing, but because of the demands of consistency and faithfulness, it causes the "old man" to come out and when that happens your "old man" says, "Well I'm not showing up for church or Bible study this time; I'll show up next time." Well, what if God did you like that? What if you prayed and He didn't answer? What if He said, "Well, I'm not showing up this time; I'll show up next week?" Well, thank God that He doesn't do that, so why should we? I'm saying all this to pull us into what we are going to discuss in the preceding chapters of this book.

Let's go to Exodus, Chapter 23. God shown me some exciting things out of these Scriptures and we are just going to roll with it.
Ex. 23: 20-23 says:

> Behold, I send an Angel before thee, to keep thee in the way, and to bring thee into the place which I have prepared (v20). Beware of him, and obey his voice, provoke him not; for he will not pardon your transgressions: for my name is in him (v 21). But if thou indeed obey his voice, and do all that I speak, then I will be an enemy to thine enemies, and an adversary unto thine adversaries (v 23).

We'll cover some things about the other verses a little bit later, but for right now I want you to understand that twice He mentioned something they needed to do. Twice He said **OBEY MY VOICE.** Let's not focus right now on God being an enemy to your enemies and an adversary to your adversaries **if you are not willing to obey His voice.** Notice the Scripture:

> (1 Sam. 15:22) And Samuel said, "Hath the LORD as great delight in burnt offerings and sacrifices as in obeying the voice of the LORD? Behold, to obey is better than sacrifice, and to hearken than the fat of rams."

Forget about being able to conquer the Amalekites and the Hittites, the Amorites and all the other "ites" if you are not willing to obey His voice. What has His voice been telling you? See, God can speak, and has been speaking, but the question is, have we been listening? Or, you heard what He said, but you acted like you didn't. I used to do that. Some of you did too when you were growing up at home. Your mama would call you to come inside, but you kept on playing. You acted like you didn't hear your mother calling you, but when she said your whole name, that's when you knew you had better get yourself on in there. Why do we have to wait until a threat is issued; why wait until mama says "I'm going to punch your lights out if you don't hurry up and get on in here!"? Or, "don't make me have to come in there and get you"? Why wait for the fierce rage of mom to come before we yield and make up our minds to obey? But you see, even at that you went and did what mom wanted done, unwillingly.

Now a lot of this same kind of thing has spilled over into the things of God. God says, "I want you to pray." You say, "I heard You Lord, but I'm not going to do that right now because I have something else to do." And then when you get in a jam, when your back is up against the wall and you're being pressured by the enemy *(or your flesh)*, then we want to go to God. We'll want hands laid on us and oil slung everywhere. We want all kinds of good and positive things to happen.

When do we want God to move? We want Him to move "right now," and the Lord says, "But you didn't do what I asked you to do. You didn't give when I said give. Now you're before Me asking for money." You'll say, "Lord, I needed You"; and He'll say, "It didn't look like you needed Me yesterday, but now that you have received a phone call saying that you're going to be sued, you need Me." God is not and should never be used as a "get me out of trouble God" only. It should be that we would want to fellowship with the Lord always, and then when trouble comes He's there. If I am not in fellowship with Him and don't take the time to go to my place of worship and move in corporate anointing, then I have a problem, and this could be the reason why things are not happening, because I've backed-up a couple of steps either intentionally or unintentionally. And, I will be honest with you; actually the Lord was on my case the other day. He spoke to me and said that I needed to step-it-up in regards to my praying and in time spent with Him. In my mind, I said, "Lord, I don't have enough time." He said, "Well hey, it's not

My fault." Again I said, "Lord, I have a lot on my schedule." He said, "Well, who scheduled it?"

We set our own schedules, God doesn't. Well, Lord I have this to do and that to do. The Lord understands that but hey, you want Him to do something for you – right? Well here is a news flash – God has already done everything He's going to do; IT IS UP TO YOU and me to do something with the tools given us. By the way, isn't God the one that blessed you with what you have? Yes, of course. Then at least we should make time to talk with Him, right? The reason we fail at this is because we are not obedient. God will tell us something - and you know He is just saying get back to where you're doing what I said, the way I said it, and that's all we're supposed to do.

You may be excellent at whatever you do for a living; the best, but it was God that blessed you with those skills and abilities. The Bible says, "For ye are brought with a price; therefore, glorify God in your body, and in your spirit, which are God's" (1 Cor. 6:20). In other words, when you buy a road map, that map now belongs to you and you're expecting that map to direct you. Another example would be the military. Once you sign on the dotted line, you now belong to whatever branch of the armed forces you've enlisted in. They have the right to tell you when to eat, sleep, wake up, what clothes to wear, etc. Why? Because now they own you – you are not your own, you gave up your own rights to serve. Well, what do you think about your and my position in God? He bought us, expecting us to work a certain way. So when you say, "I'm not going to church" (knowing that God owns you and is telling you to go) God says, "Well, wait a minute now, John 3:16 says, 'For God so loved the world He gave...' I gave Jesus. I enlisted you in My armed forces; you signed when you accepted Jesus as your Lord and Savior. I OWN YOU.

I have need of you." Don't ever think God doesn't need you. Let me take a side journey here – in 1 Cor. 12:21 it says:

"And the eye cannot say unto the hand, I have no need of thee; nor again the **head** to the feet, I have no need of you."

I used to hear people say, "God doesn't need you; He can do whatever He wants to do; He's God." Well, as you can see, the Bible says, "Don't let the head say to the foot, 'I have no need of thee'." Isn't Jesus the head? So why would He not need you? Keep in mind that He paid for your life. He paid for your existence, and it's not right for us to do what we want to do. What if you go home and all your clothes decide that they're going to get up and walk out? Hey, number one, I would let them keep right on walking. I'm not putting them on again. Whatever you buy, machinery, clothing, or furniture, you expect it to work the way it was designed to work. Well, God said He bought us and so our life is not our own; so your life now, is to serve Him. Well, if in that servitude He says, "Okay, I want you at a certain church and I want you to do what needs to be done to help fulfill that church's vision," it happens too many times we say we have too much to do or (famous two words: one starts with an "I" and the other one starts with a "T") that is, *I'm tired.* Who isn't? I mean, we all live in a fast paced society where everything is quick. I remember back in the day we used to have to turn on the TV at least 15 to 20 minutes early so the dials and stuff could warm up to a watch a program. Some of you don't know about that. That is all right! Praise the Lord! It's my job to serve Him; I am supposed to serve God. Now, if you don't want to serve God, then don't; but don't play the game. Don't go to church, don't read the Bible, and don't pray to Him. You know, when sinners get in trouble the first thing they say is, "God help." Why should He? He will, when they turn their lives over to Him; God will help – when His child prays – and will intercede for the sinner. Yes, He'll move right on in there and many have been blessed that way. I don't want to wait until something bad happens, and now here I come running, trotting to God.

You know it's astounding, when we lose our houses or lose our jobs we are on our faces before God. But then once we get our jobs back (in fact a better one) or somewhere new to live, we don't give God the time of day, because we're doing all right. As stated before in a previous illustration, God is not a "get me out of trouble, help me in this situation" type God. He is an all time God. He is to be first at all times. So when we were being disobedient, the Amorites and the Hittites and all the other "ites" were beating us to a pulp while we were trying to figure out what's going on. First, I will bring this to your attention because I don't want to be misunderstood in what I've ministered to you (the reader) so far. The Bible talks about the angel bringing us to a place and it mentions that he brought us to the Amalekites, the Hittites and so on and so forth, who are our enemies, right? Now the only reason He took us there was because the enemy was there with our belongings. The enemy was in Canaan where the land flowed with milk and honey. They have your things so you're going to have to engage in combat. You want the big grape; you're going to have to fight those dudes. You want the land; you're going to have to fight. This is very, very important. As I looked more closely at this Scripture I thought, "Well, He said you have to obey His word."

We need to be obedient. The Word of God says He sent an angel before us and He says to obey his voice and don't provoke him. The children of Israel obeyed the voice of God, the voice of the angel, but then there came a time when they didn't obey and they provoked him, and as a result they paid the price; a big price. The cost of disobedience could mean your life; it's very serious. God has always been serious. I would like to make mention of this to you since we are looking at obedience.

Romans 5:19 says:

> For as by one man's disobedience were many made sinners, so by the obedience of one shall many be made righteous.

Thank God for the obedience of Jesus! The First Adam disobeyed, and through his disobedience many were made sinners. Who are you obeying, sin or righteousness?

Romans 6:16 says:

> Know ye not, that to whom ye yield yourselves servants to obey, his servants ye are to whom ye obey; whether of sin unto death, or of obedience unto righteousness?

We are the righteousness of God, so we must obey. He didn't ask us to obey. It's not a request; it's a commandment. He didn't ask you to love one another; it's a commandment to love. Now the question is: Will we obey? Oh, this is a good one:

2 Corinthians 10:3-6 says:

> For though we walk in the flesh, we do not war after the flesh; (v4) (For the weapons of our warfare are not carnal, but mighty through God to the pulling down of strongholds;) (v5) Casting down imaginations, and every high thing that exalteth itself against the knowledge of God and bringing into captivity every thought to the obedience of Christ; (v6) And having in a readiness to revenge all disobedience, when your obedience is fulfilled.

Do you see that disobedience will not be dealt with until obedience has been done?

I Peter 2:21says:

> For even hereunto were ye called: because Christ also suffered for us, leaving us an example, that ye should follow his steps.

All right, "Jesus suffered for us, leaving us an example that we should follow in His steps." Wherever Jesus steps is where we should follow. If Jesus didn't step there, then we have no business stepping there. Where did he step? All right, we're going to find one area in which he stepped. The Bible says, "... Christ also suffered...", right?

Hebrews 5:8 says:

Though he were a Son, yet learned He obedience by the things which He suffered:

Wait a minute, what did that say, "Though He were a Son, yet learned He obedience by the things which He suffered?" Jesus learned how to obey God by what He went through. Well, so will we if we're stepping where He stepped. Just because you're going through something, doesn't mean that God is testing you; God is not testing you. Jesus was without sin, yet He was tempted, and He was tested and tried. The Devil may be mighty, but he's not all mighty. We just read that the "... weapons of our warfare are not carnal, but mighty through God to the pulling down of strongholds...." God has already given us the tools we need to come against the Amorites and the Malakites and all the other "ites", so let's use them. You have trouble? Let's get ready to rumble; pull out all your weaponry. The Word of God is our instructions. You're going to suffer, but you have to learn. There was something else that truly encouraged me - **God leads me there not only to destroy them, but because the Amorites, the Malakites, all the other "ites", have my inheritance.** God wants us to take back our inheritance; go and get your stuff, don't let the enemy have it.

Chapter
2

THE PROCESS CONTINUES

Obeying God's Voice – Part 2

And afterwards Moses and Aaron went in, and told Pharaoh, "Thus saith the LORD God of Israel, 'Let my people go, that they may hold a feast unto me in the wilderness' ". And Pharaoh said, "Who *is* the LORD that I should obey his voice to let Israel go? I know not the LORD, neither will I let Israel go (v 2)".

Exodus 5:1-2

The Lord brought this Scripture to my attention because at times, with our actions, we've said the same thing Pharaoh said. The Lord says to do this or do that and we've said with our actions and sometimes with our words, "Who is the LORD, that I should obey His voice....?" Have you ever dealt with a person you didn't like and you knew that they didn't like you, and yet God spoke to you through the Holy Sprit and said, "I want you to buy that person something nice," and you said, "Get thee behind me"? See, you didn't want to do it and you probably didn't do it. "I don't think it's fair." Nobody asked you about what's fair. We are not talking about what's fair. We are talking about what's right. We are talking about what's going to preserve your life. *Obedience! Obedience!* Exodus 19:3-5 says:

And Moses went up unto God, and the LORD called unto him out of the mountain, saying, Thus shalt thou say to the house of Jacob, and tell the children of Israel: (v 4)Ye have seen what I did unto the Egyptians, and how I bear you on eagles' wings, and brought you unto Myself. (v 5) Now therefore, if ye will obey My voice indeed, and keep my covenant, then ye shall be a peculiar treasure unto Me above all people; for all the earth is Mine:

Now, I want to mention something to you here; if you'll notice we can go through a whole lot of Scriptures in the Old Testament that speak about obeying His voice. Now, this is what He is really saying: "The children of Israel, when they were in Egypt didn't hear my voice". In fact, when they were coming out of Egypt, following the plagues, God wanted to stop speaking to them through all the outward signs, demonstrations, and manifestations as before; He wanted them to hear and "Obey My voice"; not see pillars of fire by night, and the cloud by day. He wanted to talk to them and for them to talk to Him, and that's why they had to go three days journey out from Egypt. And when they reached Mt. Sinai, the thundering and lightning and the smoke was the voice of God up there, and the children of Israel said, "Moses, speak thou with us, and we will hear, but let not God speak with us least we die," (Ex. 20:18-19). God wanted them to come and sanctify themselves; get before the base of the mountain so that they could hear Him for themselves, but they would not because they were afraid, they thought would perish. But all God was trying to do was train them to hear His voice; not look for signs, but to hear the voice!

Here we saw how the Word of God worked in the Old Testament and we can see God's Word work through His Son, Jesus Christ, in the New Testament, and all of it pertains to hearing "*His voice.*" You are able to hear God at your house. You don't actually have to go to church; however, we should go to church. You could've heard God as soon as you were dismissed from service, in your car or walking home, whatever you do. You can talk and fellowship with God. Jesus put us back in the position of the First Adam.   Adam and Eve walked and communed with God in the cool of the Garden of Eden, but there came a time when even they disobeyed God. God told them not to eat of "The Tree of Life".   God spoke this to Adam. Eve's last name was Adam also (Mr and Mrs Adam). God said, "But of the tree of knowledge of good and evil, thou shall not eat of it:..." and once woman was created, Adam was to give her the same instructions. It was not an apple tree. It was just a tree they weren't supposed to eat of. And so Eve started looking at the tree desiring it (Gen. 3:6). This is how the enemy works: he'll entice you to look at things that you know you shouldn't be looking at, and walk by things you shouldn't be walking by.   Although the Lord has delivered you from that sin *(and you are now a Christian),* it doesn't mean that you have to go back in sin. Once you have been born again, rooted and grounded in His Word, God may want you to go back to help other people out of what you were in, but it may not be at the very beginning of your walk with God. You see, you may have been a Christian for a short while and you may think that you're ready to go back, but you're not. But the Bible says in Philippians 4:13:

"I can do all things through Christ which strengtheneth me."

Yes, you can do all things through Christ, but you may not know enough - and the next thing you know, the enemy will plant a thought in your mind that'll have you thinking how nice it would be just to look at, or go by there, to touch and feel again (so on and so forth). "Just one more time; it's not going to hurt anything; just one more time." You can ask for forgiveness afterwards. Don't put yourself in positions that you know you're not strong enough to be in. Cast down every thought and imagination that the enemy brings (2 Cor. 10:4-6). Let me make it plain, and give you an example: You're single and a member of your church, who happens to be male and single, says to you, "We need to pray: come over to my house." You agree and go. You have just put yourself in a situation you do not need to be in. The scenario is, woman and man together with the intention of coming together to pray for one another ("We're just going to pray"). And you expect nothing to happen? Even though there may be no mutual interest one towards the other, it won't matter when you get together and you start holding hands- talking about "let's just touch and agree." What are you about to touch? Go to your church or have prayer in the company of others because you'll be doing a whole lot more than praying if you succumb to thoughts planted by the enemy. Some people might say, "I don't have problems like that." However, the Bible says, *"don't let your good be evil spoken of"* (Rom. 14:16). You don't know yourself as well as you think you do and neither does anybody else. If somebody had a shot gun pointed at you right now and said, "If you say you believe in Christ, I'll shoot you," what do you do? Some would say, "I'd stand on the Word." That's the right answer, but you don't know if you would do that. You probably wouldn't be able to move! I've seen big, strong, adult men run from mice! You only know what you should do. It's like being pushed to your max and you did or said something that you never thought you would do or say again. This is why we must put the Word of God into our hearts so that the Word will rise up and overtake our thoughts and actions.

We must get to a point where we know ourselves well *enough to predict our actions* (Heb. 5:14). How can you get to know yourself? How will you know what you need to deny? - When you get in the Word. The Word will show you who you are in

Christ, and where you are and what you must do. You shouldn't get upset when you're not producing like you should. You just need to get in there and find out what you're missing. What am I not doing? See, there is nothing wrong with the Word of God. There's something wrong with the ones who operate it. In other words, the Word of God operates as it was designed to do, according to the will of God.

When I first learned how to play the keyboard I used to come home from school and practice for four hours everyday on songs of gospel artists that had the hardest music around- like Andre Crouch and other and the like. I didn't even know how to read musical notes. I'd just sit there and rehearse the songs, trying to play them. Once I learned how to play them I would play them with my eyes closed but in a different key all the way through without messing up. Then I would go up a half note and try to learn it in that key and after a while I was able to play those songs in any key, but it took practice. You cannot pray and believe God, then put your hands on a keyboard and expect success when you haven't studied or done anything. Joshua 24:20:

> If ye forsake the LORD, and serve strange gods, then He will turn and do you hurt, and consume you, after He hath done you good.

You have to understand, God does not bring hurt to you, but He will move out of the way while the enemies bring hurt to you; all the **"ites"** will hurt you. Continuing with (verses 21-24):

> (v-21) And the people said unto Joshua, "Nay; but we will serve the LORD". (v-22) And Joshua said unto the people, "Ye are witnesses against yourselves that ye have chosen the LORD, to serve Him". And they said, "We are witnesses". (v-23) "Now therefore put away the strange gods which are among you, and incline your heart unto the LORD God of Israel". (v-24) And the people said unto Joshua, "the LORD our God will we serve, and His voice will we obey".

If you choose to serve the Lord, then you are a witness against yourself. Keep on reading. As it goes into (v 28) it says:

> (v-28) So Joshua let the people depart, every man unto his inheritance.

In other words, they said, "we're going to serve the Lord and we're going to do what God says." So He said okay now you're free to go and take up what is rightfully yours. But you cannot take it if there is no **obedience**. I'll repeat that, you cannot take what is rightfully yours if you don't obey. Don't make it so hard. Some people make serving God so rigid that when they overlook something, or make a mistake; they'll beat themselves up so bad that there is no room for recovery.

In the Book of Acts, Chapter 5:29 says:

> "...We ought to obey God rather than men."

People have taken part of this verse and just run completely crazy with it, rendering a mindset of "the Bible tells me to obey God rather than man, so I don't have to listen to you; I don't have to do anything you say." Is that what He said? Because if that's true, then why did He also say (Heb. 13:17), "Obey them that have rule over you..." Why did He say that? What's up with that?

So when we take things out of context our thinking becomes convoluted and confused, and we form ideas that are strange. You will come up with some of the most ridiculous things if you're not careful.

You'll make up things that God didn't say because in order to hear the voice of God, and know that it is God, takes skill and practice. That's why we're supposed to pray in the Holy Spirit and then sit there, keeping ourselves quiet so that we can hear what He's saying. A lot of people don't pray in the Holy Spirit everyday, only when things get bad or when things don't look right. You may ask, "Can I just talk to God?" Yes you can. But there are some who believe God cannot speak to you. Everyone that says God cannot speak to you usually believes that you can pray to God. So, you mean to tell me that we can do something God cannot do? That doesn't make sense, does it? You can talk to Him, but He cannot talk to you. He can hear you, but you cannot hear Him.

I was engaged in conversation with somebody one time, actually this was years ago, and they were telling me that they would like to see (written in black and white or red) specific Scriptures on what the Bible says about this or that or the other. Most of the time there may not be one verse in particular that describes that thing you're believing or needing an answer to. Whatever it is it may not be in that one particular verse, but in a combination of multiple verses. For instance, some may ask, "Where does it say in the Bible to love thy neighbor as yourself?" Well, you can find that; however, there may not be "one" Scripture that explains how Satan was god of this world in times past. You'd have to get several Scriptures, from Genesis to Revelation, and pull them all together. I'm telling you right now, when you spend time with God you will come to know Him; you'll know exactly what He says. It all goes along with the flow of the Book.

Before, I've said you cannot preach on salvation and then say salvation is for everybody, and then on the other hand say healing is not for everybody; healing is in salvation. So, you see it all has to flow; everything has to flow. If you study on the Father, if you study on the Son (Jesus), if you study on healing, if you study on faith, if you study on the righteousness of God, if you study on dispensations, if you study on any of these subjects it all has to fit. You cannot say in one area that you're saved (Are you saved? Yeah I'm saved! Well praise the Lord!), then say in another area, "Are you righteous?" "No, there's none righteous, no not one." "It's in the Bible." Yeah, but you didn't read it correctly. You cannot be saved and not be righteous. The Bible says, "You are the righteousness of God." It all has to fit, so don't go running off talking about, "I don't need to listen to anybody."

There is more Scripture, 1 John 2:20-27 where it says, "But the anointing which ye have received of Him abideth in you, and ye need not that any man teach you...." Now what does that mean? That means if no one can teach you, then what is the purpose of Ministry? You could stay home in your bed on Sundays and just open your Bible and say, "Okay Lord teach me. Teach me Lord, teach me!" You don't need to have a church home.

It's really not talking about you getting all the teaching for yourself to where you don't need anybody. It's not saying that you don't need to obey people; you're obeying somebody. Again, if you didn't obey your mama, you were reprimanded; also when you became of a certain age and thought you were grown and rebelled when your mother disciplined you. You were flexing your little muscles and were like, "Yeah come on." You did that only until your daddy came home. Now that you are out on your own (you're grown), *you still have to obey somebody.* If you're working for somebody they tell you when to show up for work and when not too. If you have your own business you still have guidelines and timelines to obey. Say you need to go get paper from the store and they're closed. Well, you cannot make them open the store. Obey the time; you cannot get around it. *So let's obey God.*

Romans 6:12 says:

> Let not sin therefore reign in your mortal body, that ye should obey it in the lusts thereof.

We do not need to obey our bodies; our bodies are not born again. Continuing with verses 13 and 14 it says:

> Neither yield to your members as instruments of unrighteousness unto sin: but yield yourselves unto God, as those that are alive from the dead, and your members as instruments of righteousness unto God. For sin shall not have dominion over you: for ye are not under the law, but under grace.

Let's substitute the word Satan for sin. "... Satan shall not have dominion over you ...." Let's continue:

> (v15) What then? shall we sin, because we are not under the law but, under grace? God forbid. (v16) Know ye not that to whom ye yield yourselves servants to obey, his servants ye are to whom ye obey; whether of sin unto death, or of **obedience** to righteousness?.

I hope you catch this. *Obedience* moves you into an area of right-standing with God. Disobedience moves you into an area of death. So if I want to continue to operate in the righteousness or rights that I have in Christ, then I must be obedient! My flesh does not want to hear it, but I have to be obedient. There was a time when the Lord instructed me to go do something for someone and I didn't feel like it. I didn't get goose bumps as an indication that the anointing was on me to move; there wasn't any of that! I was tired; didn't want to go! My wife said, "Let's go" *(you see she was hearing from God, I wasn't – I was too tired)*. I said, "No". She said, "Well I'm going, and you are too." Thank God for her boldness, and thank God I went anyway, and because we were OBEDIENT in spite of how either of us felt, the Lord moved mightily that day! It had nothing to do with what I or my wife felt.

You have to do things when you don't feel like it. You have to give when you think you don't have it to give. I'm going to repeat that one more time. You have to give (not just money) and you have to give when you think you don't have it to give. I was listening to Dr. Fredrick K. C. Price the other day and he was talking about giving, and it really moved me. He asked a question along this line: how many of you could use $643,000.000?

You could use it right? He said that's what he and his wife gave away last year. I started thinking about that and I said "Well, what did I give away last year?" I didn't know. I started thinking. The Lord said, "Now listen, I've been trying to get you [though God was talking to me then, I know He's talking to all of us] to a place where you are giving more each year; the more you give the more you're going to receive."

It's some people's goal to make $43, 000.00 a year and he's giving away $643, 000.00. So this was what the Lord was telling me. He said "Look at what you're giving."

He had been trying to move me into an area of increase but you see, disobedience and fear will keep you from giving and when you don't give as God has instructed you to give, then you're disobedient and rebellious, and "... rebellion is as the sin of witchcraft...."(1 Sam. 15:23) so you've allowed all this junk to come in and keep you suppressed. Many are afraid to give because this is due and that is due, thinking, "if I give what God wants me to give now, then how am I going to pay this bill?" You don't think He knows that you have a gas bill to pay?

Listen, there have been times when we've moved out in faith (my wife and I) and we've given with our knees shaking; but when we gave because He (God) told us to, in our time of reaping we received much more than what we had given. That's how it is. All the time He is saying "I want to get you to where you can give not just $100.00, but $ 1,000.00, not just a $1,000.00 but thousands." We'll never get there if we don't trust and if we don't what? *Obey.* It is not your concern if God told you to do it- don't argue and fuss with it in your mind. **Very important: make sure that its God telling you to give don't be drawn into emotional giving.**

Now, I know a whole lot of people are going to be thinking or hoping that God won't tell them anything – and many will do their best to stay away from church, trying to stay baby Christians so as not to hear God's voice. They do not want to grow up because that means responsibility.

You know we have a tendency to sit back, claiming that God hasn't said anything to us. You have to make sure that you're not in that position in which you act like you don't hear God. See, God said, "Go ye into all the world and preach the Gospel," so when God commissions a ministry to do outreach work within the community or in other countries overseas, if we can't join them there then we should do whatever we can to assist them with their efforts to help those in need. I was blessed enough to go to Russia and Brazil to help some ministries in their effort to spread the Word of God. And everyone who sent me, or had a part in sending me, to Russia and Brazil got credit for all the people that were saved and for all the people that were delivered; it's as if they were there. Because when you support other ministries and when those ministries are blessed by God you too will receive a blessing; for the Bible says, "we are one in the Body of Christ." But when we say, "I cannot do it," or "I won't do it," now you're moving into the area of disobedience.

God wants to pull us up out of that. I'm believing, (and I don't know if the Lord is going to have me speak on this extensively) He wants us accomplished enough so that we can pay our bills off with no problem or not have any bills at all! So when your church sponsors a community outreach to win souls, or a church cruise, everybody will be ready to go. I'll never forget the time my church (Church of the Redeemed) wanted to sponsor a cruise; I'm telling you people were scraping money from wherever they could scrape it from, and there were people who went that I thought would not be able to go, you know? Praise the Lord! Then when there was talk of starting a building fund for a better facility, nothing happened. The cruise meant more than the building fund. Why? The cruise was something pleasurable; the cruise was something they wanted to do, and the work of God meant nothing. Isn't that interesting? It is not only interesting, but it is sad. God, who gave you the money to go on the cruise, would have given you the money to do His work.

God has me mentioning these things to make you think. You and I have to think. Where are our priorities? Who are we serving? Who are we obeying? Who is Lord? We say, "Jesus," but out of the other side of our mouths we are saying "Satan." Could it be my job, my house, my kids, me, my car that's lord of my life, that's god of my life? Then when we get in trouble we pray and God through His mercy... We'd better be thankful for the mercy of God.

The Bible says His mercies are renewed every morning! If His mercy wasn't renewed every morning we'd be in a mess! So we have to obey Him. It's going to be hard on our flesh, but we have to obey Him. If He says "give," give it, and then thank God that you receive your reward. If He says, "pray", pray. Get busy at your local church. See to it that the Church (and its ministry) you attend is one that you are proud of. Oh, Pastor you know that the Bible says, "Pride goeth before destruction" (Prov. 16:18). But you can be proud in the right way.

I'm proud of Jesus, aren't you? Well, did you get destroyed because of that? I'm proud of my wife, and you should be proud of your wife or husband. If you don't have a spouse to be proud of, be proud of your kids, if you have them. There is nothing wrong with being proud, as long as we don't allow arrogance to dominate us, or develop a haughty spirit.

I challenge you this week to spend more time in prayer and more time in the Word of God; attend Bible study and prayer meetings. I believe in Jesus' name that there will be a difference in your life. Now you have to be consistent and be willing to do whatever God tells you to do; *be obedient.* I cannot stress that enough. Give of your tithes and offerings, and if He tells you to do something above that then, hey, we're rolling because there is something better on the way. The times I have given when God told me to give, when I didn't want to give or I felt that I didn't have what He told me to give, there was always something else on up the road that was better than what I could've ever imagined; always. Now, you have to say, "Okay Lord, I want to do this on a continual basis." I want to always tithe.

Never stop giving of tithes and offerings, but make sure you're giving offerings where He tells you to give. And just because someone may have holes in their shoes and they come show me, doesn't mean I'm going to buy them some shoes! When you see people on the street, you don't just give them money; we want to be selective and give wherever God tells us to give, whether it looks good in the eyes of other people or not, I believe, for increase in every area in my ministry, in other ministries, and in our lives.

Chapter
3

Bringing It More Together

Angels Keeping Us in the Way-Part 1

Again, we are going to Exodus 23. Verses 20-28 say,

> Behold, I send an Angel before thee, to keep thee in the way, and to bring thee into the place which I have prepared (v20). Beware of him, and obey his voice, provoke him not; for he will not pardon your transgressions: for my name is in him (v 21). But if thou shalt indeed obey his voice, and do all that I speak; then I will be an enemy to thine enemies, and an adversary unto thine adversaries (v 22). For mine Angel shall go before thee, and bring thee in unto the Amorites, the Hittites, and the Perizzites, and the Canaanites, and the Hivites, and the Jebusites: and I will cut them off (v 23). Thou shall not bow down to their gods, nor serve them, nor do after their works: but thou shalt utterly overthrow them, and quite break down their images (v24). And ye shall serve the LORD your God, and he shall bless thy bread, and thy water; and I will take sickness away from the midst of thee (v 25). There shall nothing cast their young, nor be barren, in thy land: the number of thy days I will fulfil (v 26). And I will send hornets before thee, which shall drive out the Hivites, the Canaanite, and the Hittite, from before thee (v 28).

Praise the Lord. We have been going over certain things in the Word of God out of this passage, and God has given us some good nuggets of gold. In other words, God has revealed truth to us; things that we didn't see before, we now see and He's answered a lot of questions as to the process of how the Kingdom of God operates, why things are the way they are, and why things happen.

You know we have these questions. We go through different things, and we stand on the Word of God and we pray. We've prayed and we've stood on the Word for victory and for deliverance and then other things began to happen that we didn't expect and we're like, "Well, Lord wait a minute: I didn't pray to be in this mess; now I'm in it and why is that?" We began to see here in this passage, as you look again at Exodus, 23:20:

He says He has sent an Angel before us to keep us in the way. There is a way we must go, but there is a way that must be kept, and He is going to keep us through the help of our personal angel; the angel will not only guard and protect us, but is going to (as we find out) *bring us to a place.* And many times we've prayed for God to take us to Canaan's land, but what we've failed to realize is that when we are on our way to Canaan there are tests and trials; and once we reach Canaan there are giants there and battles to be fought. And here He tells us in (v 23) that the angel shall go before us and he shall bring us unto the Amorites, the Hittites, and the Perizzites, and the Jebusites, and Hivites, and Canaanites and even Girbizites, Devilites, and Demonites (I added those last two on there – but you get the point), all of whom are our enemy. God said that He would bring you to your blessing place, but realize that all the **"ites"** are there guarding the objects or the very things that belong to us. So we're going to have to face the enemy even though a lot of times we don't want to. We want to pray and let God move him out of the way so we can just walk in free and clear, but that's not the case.

This is not a game we are playing here. The devil is not playing with you, and God has never played; it is a very serious thing, but many of us have taken it for granted and have not looked at the gravity of the matter. You have prayed and your answer has not come in full manifestation, but you can start to see certain things take shape and form. The sower sows the Word and then it comes; first the blade and then the ear and then the full corn in the ear. Sometimes it hasn't even grown into the full corn, yet you see the blade and you get excited. There is nothing wrong with getting excited, but you do not want to harvest the blade!

By going out and trying to do a whole bunch of stuff that we should not be doing sooner than we should moves us into areas that cause premature manifestation; we end up jumping the gun. We have to realize that we have enemies and I know you see that, but how many of you know that some of these "ites" are you? I'll tell you who these "ites" are that we've read about here in Exodus 23.

I'm going to give you a short commentary about the different "Ites":

The *Amorite:* the high one, highlander or mountaineer; they dwell in the high places. In other words, the Amorite dwells on the mountain top. The Bible says, "Yea though I walk through the valley of the shadow of death, I will fear no evil" (Ps. 23:4). So when we say, "we're going through," we're in a valley season; and if you are operating in fear, the Amorites will attack you from high places as you walk through the valley.

The *Hittite:* one who develops siege tactics; inventor of weapons forged from iron; are likely to create trouble for you and cordon you off in certain areas.

The *Hivites:* are internal; mid-landers, who dwell in the inward places. So now you have the highlander, which is the Amorites and the Hivites (who could be a branch of the Hittites, but these Hivites dwell in inward places).

The *Perizzites:* are villagers, grazers, farmers, and peasants, who plant things. The Bible (Matthew 13:26-28) refers to the sower who sowed a good seed, and so on and so forth, and then it mentions that the blade and the fruit appeared as well as tares, so the question was asked, "How did tares get mixed in with the wheat?" The rest of the verse says, "... an enemy hath done this......" So by definition a Perizzite may have sown bad seed; therefore, sowing negative things into our lives.

The deceptiveness of the enemy is subtle. The enemy doesn't come right out and tell you that he's going to make you a hit man for the mob, or turn a lady into a hooker, or one into a gambler; he comes in cunning and slick ways. He may start off by telling you it's OK to be angry and to yield to it over and over. Or, maybe you've selected a prospective mate, someone who gambles and looks successful and has lots money that entices you enough to want to be like them. For example: I used to think that when I went to a grocery store or a clothing store and purchased an item and the cashier made an error in giving me too much change back that it was all right for me to keep it. I would walk out of the store (and I did this in all sincerity because I just didn't know any better) thinking, "Thank You Lord for blessing me." I actually thought that the cashier's mistake was a blessing from God when I knew that they didn't charge the correct price for the item! The Lord didn't bless me; I was deceived into thinking that He did. Now, keep this in mind, if I'm totally unaware of the situation and/or transaction, that's something different.

It's not any different than eating fruit in the produce area that you haven't paid for. But by now you have graduated from taking stuff from the store to falsifying your tax returns; lying to your boss; stealing from work. You're supposed to be there at a designated time and you arrive when you get ready and leave before you should leave when you really haven't worked the entire time, nor made up any time.

You know when you eat something very hot and scorch your tongue real bad, you can still eat but you can't taste anything for a while? Well, it's the same thing spiritually. You have evolved to where your conscience, which is your spirit man, is now scorched (1Tim. 4:2). If you continue this way, your spirit man will become so seared that the Holy Spirit won't say anything to you because you are insensitive to God's voice.

Because you've practiced this type of behavior for so long, when you try to sow good seed the dishonest seed will grow too, and now you have mixed seeds: good seeds and bad seeds. The enemy now has something to use. The *Perizzites* have come in and sown that seed, and you left it there unchecked so now it's growing and you're wondering why you have mingled seed- "....*The enemy hath done this.*" Then the next thing you know you've been prepped for a major theft that you feel is a deal you cannot refuse and so you compromise and say, "Okay, well maybe I can do this just this once."

It's never just "this one time." It's never just once at the slot machine; you'll be there all night hoping you hit big. Even when people win money they will stay there until they lose it all; it's all deception. Let me mention the other "ites".

The *Jebusites:* a sect from the Canaanites; one who treads or tramples; they loathe you; they want you under their feet. (Incidentally all the "ites" are a spin off or a sect of the Canaanites). The Bible says that the "enemy is under our feet."

(Eph 1:22) And hath put all things under his feet, and gave him to be the head over all things to the church,

Jesus is the Head and we are the body; everything is under His feet, which means everything is under our feet - so we shouldn't be under their feet.

The *Canaanites:* merchants and traffickers; to bend beneath, to humiliate, to vanquish, to bring down into subjection. Therefore, the Canaanite's job is to use all the other "ites" to get you to bend the knee in defeat, submitting yourself to them. You're getting hit from high places, you're getting hit from the inside, someone is stepping on you, and the pressure increases to where you give up and bow to their gods.

God is showing us the process of how the enemy tries to get to us, and how we can come out against them. We can do all things through Christ, (the Anointed), who strengthens us (Philip. 4:13).

We read in Ex. 23:24

Ye shall not bow down to their gods

So when we come face-to-face with the "ites", even though we're getting hit from the top, the sides, the back, and the front, *do not bow down!* We are strong enough, we have the Word of God, the Name of Jesus, and all of the angels of God – so *do not bow!* When the pressure is on, it will seem easier to give in, but there are consequences; woe be unto us when or if we give in. That could be the time when the answer comes into manifestation, or when Jesus returns. I used to think I was smart enough from the Word of God to think Jesus cannot come right now because the Bible says, "He's coming back for a church without spot or blemish." Spots and blemishes can be people. Spots and blemishes are sins and iniquities. When you look at the Body of Christ, everybody has issues or something going on. The Lord asked me, "How do you know that I couldn't give a revelation to everybody (in the Body of Christ) at the exact same time that could bring about deliverance in their lives while you're out messing around?" I didn't think about that! God could send a revelation to some in a dream, others something in a vision, in your prayer time or during your study time. He has many avenues. He can come anytime; that's why the Bible says, (Eph. 4:26) "Be ye angry, and sin not; let not the sun go down on upon your wrath." Why? You don't know when Jesus is coming. I used to think, "Well, Lord you don't know what they did." Can you imagine telling the Lord He doesn't know what they did? Sometimes we can get so caught up in our situations that we say things to God that just don't make sense.

Note in these passages of Scripture, that we've read it tells us in a couple of them one thing. In Ex. 23:21 it says, "Beware of him and obey his voice," and in verse 22 "But if thou shall indeed obey his voice, then I will be an enemy to your enemies." Only when we obey will He be an "adversary to our adversaries." When you have not been obedient, you can say all you want to say and what you're saying can be true and right; nevertheless, if you're not obedient it's not going to work. If you've decided to take a route other than the one the angel who went before you prepared, you've compounded the problem. Why would you go a way that is unprepared?

Though you were going the wrong way, you prayed to God to help you, and the angel is doing all he can to get your attention. Why do we usually do the opposite of what we are told to do? Why is it when I pray, I'm still in the same trouble? Why is it when I pray, it gets worse? The reason is, you have been placed in front of the "ites"; the angel brought you there, and the "ites" are trying to keep you from receiving the blessings of God.

But praise God you made it this far because while you were on the journey the enemy was trying to do things to get you to transgress and sin; but you made it to the "place" and now you're at that "place," but what's up with these enemies? These are things that you have to deal with. A lot of times the "ites" aren't the "Devil or the enemy," it is us. Here's how I know: As the children of Israel were coming out of Egypt they were in the wilderness, and while they were there a variety of things happened. In retrospect, the wilderness is a type of your flesh: emotions, and feelings. It is all these inward things that you are unaware of. You have an idea of what you think you would do, as well as what you should do. If the Word has not been planted and rooted in you, more than likely you will do what you should not do even though you know better.

If somebody overheard you say that you loved the Lord and you'd serve Him with all your might, and they later asked you to smoke a joint with them for old time's sake, more than likely you would say, "No, I'm not smoking that because that isn't of the Lord." Then the circumstances change drastically: someone with a gun demands that you smoke the joint and renounce Jesus. Now what would you do? While you are sitting in your comfort zone, you can think of all the right answers until you are face-to-face with a mad man and you hear that "click-click" of the gun. Now what are you going to do?

What I'm saying is, we must stay in the Word. Obedience is greater than sacrifice. How many times have we gone to our local place of assembly and in our homes and brought forth the sacrifice of praise? Unfortunately, it is not a sacrifice unless there's been obedience first. You have to obey the Lord. Now that you've learned about tithing, give of your tithe and of your offering. The pattern should be: the next time you get paid; give of your tithes and offerings and thereafter, so on and so forth. Yet, when you give, you don't see anything happening. Could it be because you're making a sacrifice without obedience? God will not receive your offering.

The tithe belongs to God; however, the offering is an offer you are making to God and God, if it is not presented to Him properly according to His Word will refuse your offer. Yet you are still trying to offer a sacrifice to God. What was the last thing God told you to do? (I'm talking about you individually). What did God put in your heart? What instructions were you to follow? Maybe God wanted you to pray right away for whatever reason, and you decided not to (*here is another area of deception*). You decided you would pray later; it's too late. That's disobedience. We are so used to doing things when we want to, when we feel like it, and when it's convenient.

Now if God leaves it open for you to do it whenever it is convenient for you, wonderful! Example: He said "when you fast"; He didn't tell you to fast on a specific day, or at a specific time; he left it open to you and me (unless specified). When He tells you specifically to do things, you are going to have to do what He says. I've tried this and I'm sure you have too; I was disobedient to God, and then I tried to read the Bible and I could not get a thing out of it; no revelation. The only thing that kept coming up was what I should have done. Just think about it. I needed to move in obedience.

Chapter
4

Following Your Angel

Obeying the Angel Sent Before You

Your Bible is the Word of God; use His Word and apply it to your everyday life.

I am just giving you what God has given me. I have to be obedient to the Spirit of God. I believe a multitude of questions that you may have had, or others that may have come to mind, may have been answered by now. I realize that you have been doing some digesting and processing because the Word of God is always true and enlightening. I discovered more things in Exodus 23:20-30

> Behold, I send an Angel before thee, to keep thee in the way, and to bring thee into the place which I have prepared (v20). Beware of him, and obey his voice, provoke him not; for he will not pardon your transgressions: for my name is in him (v21). But if thou shalt indeed obey his voice, and do all that I speak; then I will be an enemy unto thine enemies and an adversary unto thine adversaries (v22). For mine Angel shall go before thee, and bring thee in unto the Amorites, and the Hittites, and the Perizzites, and the Canaantes, the Hivites, and the Jebusites: and I will cut them off (v23). Thou shalt not bow down to their gods, nor serve them, nor do after their works: but thou shalt utterly overthrow them, and quite break down their images (v24). And ye shall serve the LORD your God, and he shall bless thy bread, and thy water; and I will take sickness away from the midst of thee (v25). There shall nothing cast their young, [in other words women will have children and they won't miscarry] nor be barren, in thy land: the number of thy days I will fulfill (v26). I will send my fear before thee, and will destroy all the people to whom thou shall come, and I will make all thine enemies turn their backs unto thee (v27). And I will send hornets before thee, which shall drive out the Hivite, the Canaanite, and the Hittite from before thee (v28). I will not

drive them out from before thee in one year; lest the land become desolate, and the beast of the field multiply against thee (v29). By little and little [or little by little] I will drive them out from before thee, until thou be increased, and inherit the land (v30).

He does not say He might drive them out He says, He will drive them out! I don't know about you, but I've already preached myself happy! Glory to God! I want you to notice something that I hadn't noticed before. I want you to observe the wording; look at what He says in verse 20:

"Behold, I send an Angel before thee to keep thee....." or to guard thee or to protect thee. We need to be kept; "... keep thee in the way and bring thee into a place..." that He has prepared. An angel has gone before us; God has enough of them to give to everybody. According to the Bible, He has so many that no man can number (Rev. 5:11); compared with (Heb. 12:22), an innumerable company of angels, is what God has. If we were to figure it out, we have a minimum of forty thousand angels apiece and when you study the Word of God you'll discover that angels are not 5 feet tall; they're not 3 feet tall either, with little wings and a bow and arrow. They are tall, strong, and mighty. One angel killed one hundred and eighty-five thousand men in one night! And you have at least forty thousand and they move as fast as lightning.

I heard someone speak once on sound and light, time and space, and as he was speaking I thought to myself it's true, the speed of light was something that God set into motion. Right? He said "Let there be light," and when He said it, it went out, one hundred and eighty-six thousand miles per second or faster. Universes are being created just as fast. If angels move as fast as lightning, realize this: God can move even faster!

Now this is science; when you look out into the darkness at night and you see the stars twinkling, most of the time that star has already vanished and all we're seeing is the residual effect of a star that has burned out thousands of years ago; that's one way of explaining how fast light travels. Now if that just applies to the stars, which is only the second heaven, then how did Jesus die, go to heaven, and come back? See how fast God moves? Can you grasp how fast He can change you, how fast He can straighten you and me out? Your situation, your circumstance! He said "Behold, I send an Angel". Now I keep going over this because as we go through these next verses it's going to hit you. "Behold, I send an Angel before thee, to keep thee in the way [this indicates that there is a certain way we are to go] and to bring thee into the place [or bring you to the place] which I have prepared." Then it says, "Beware of him, and obey his voice...." this means he's going to talk to you. Don't try to figure out whether it's Jesus talking to you, whether it's the Holy Ghost talking to you, or whether it's the angel talking to you; that's irrelevant. Just receive from God. If He says "stop," you stop; if He says "go," you go. But you better make sure it's Him. In 1 Corinthians 14:10 it says,

"There are, it may be so many kinds of voices in the world, and none of them is without significance."

In other words, there are voices that are speaking all the time; talking to us. You not only have to look at what the Word of God says, but you have to examine what it doesn't say because it's there. Everything has a voice; it talks. The fig tree talked to Jesus (Mark 11:12-13); it said I had figs. It was time for figs and when Jesus went there to eat of them it didn't have any and the Bible says "...and Jesus answered and said...." You don't answer something unless it talks to you. I'll give you another good example: your bills talk to you. You don't see a mouth on the envelope, but they have a voice, and I'll be honest with you and tell you this: most of the time when God is speaking to you, you don't want to do what He says because it's a chastisement, a correction, a rebuke, or a reproof. He speaks to us in love this way because He's trying to get us to a place. All right here we go- so we have to obey His voice. Why? Because: His name is in Him.

Then verse 22 says:

> But if thou indeed obey his voice, and do all that I speak; then will I be an enemy unto thine enemies, and adversary unto thine adversaries [here it is]. (v23) For mine Angel shall [do what?] go before thee, and bring thee unto [who?] the Amorities......

Remember (verse 21) says:

"Behold, I send an Angel before thee," and he's going to guard you and protect you along this way, and he's going to bring you to a place. The place that he is going to bring you to is to your enemy. I didn't make it up; its right here in the text. The Amorites, the Canaanites, the Jebusites, the Hittites, the Hivites, and the Perizzites are our enemies. What I'm about to point out is not contrary to anything I've ever taught before in my ministry or in the writing of this book. God will prove this to you from His Word, and you're going to have to pay close attention to it.

We've been on our knees praying to the Lord for help and the Lord has replied with, "Okay now, I'm going to take you to a place." Now the "place" has been misconstrued in our minds as this wonderful, happy haven where we'll just be at rest; because we've imagined that's what God would do, and for that reason the Devil has been whooping our heads. In [v20] God said the angels' going to bring you to a "place," but in [v23] there is a more detailed explanation of where the angel is going to bring you. Take note: "For mine Angel shall go before thee, and bring thee unto the Amorites, the Hittites, and the Perizzites...:" all those "ites", even the Devilites and Demonites [my addition], and He said He would cut them off. Look at [v24]: "Thou shall not bow down to their gods...." Listen, if you need to be set free from something you have to get on your knees before God, because the angel has already gone before you! He went before you so that he could bring you to that "something" you need to be set free of. You follow me?

He's guarding you and me, protecting us all the way up to that moment when we are facing the "ites." Things may come from all directions, trying to keep you out of the "way," but God says "No! Keep going!" Then why does all of that stuff you were trying to suppress and keep down, surface? Because it needs to be cut off. Look at the rest of verse 24:

"...nor serve them, nor do after their works: but [what?] "thou [thou is you] shalt utterly overthrow them and quite break down their images".

You shall break down their images when the angel brings you to the "place." Not the La-de-da retreat, but to your enemy; to the real you. When the angel brings you to face the virtues and vices within, you have to come out against them; you have to overthrow them, you have to break them down. It is at this moment, when the angel brings you to that "place", God tells you don't kneel down and be subservient to the same mess that keeps you in bondage; where you were. God said don't yield to it again because the next time you pray He's going to take you right back there again. Glory! You have to get this. He's going to bring you- not to La-de-da Island; but before your enemies and you have to deal with them or get dealt with.

Praise the Lord! Look at verse 25: "And ye shall [do what?] serve the LORD your God, and he shall bless thy bread, and thy water;....." and the sickness will be taken away from our midst **WHEN WE STOP BOWING DOWN**.

We've been asking this question: "Lord I've been standing on Your Word, and why is this happening? Or, I've sowed seeds and given my tithes - why are my finances worse?" This is why. We're supposed to break down the images. You and I have the authority to smash them. They had the authority in the Old Testament, so you know for a fact we have that same or more authority in the New Testament. We're supposed to come out against our enemy to the point where our enemy's back is to us and not the opposite where your back is turned to the enemy. Don't run from the Devil and then talk about how you have the Devil on the run. Is he running after you or are you running after him?

Chapter
5

Don't' Give Up

Be Not Deceived

The Lord wants me to share this with you, "Don't give up". One of the greatest things the enemy does is to get you in a state of discouragement. The Lord has been dealing with me on this subject and His words to me were, that His people have a tendency to give up too quickly; we slow down and decrease in committing to as much, or just give up, period. It can get tough. Now don't misunderstand me; we're all on the front line, and we're getting hit with everything the enemy has.

At first, it seemed as though money was an issue and you could deal with everything else; secondly he tried to afflict you with sickness; he tried to mess with your job. Now he has the dog running you crazy! Just one thing after another; however, the Bible says, "Be strong in the Lord and the power of His might." **His might,** not yours.

Spiritually speaking, there may be somebody behind you (rank wise: in knowledge and experience with God) on the battle field. I remember when I was behind the people that were *(spiritually ahead of me)* on the front lines; they were more knowledgeable of God's Word and skillful in the word of righteousness, but every once in a while a fiery dart from the enemy would slip through and I'd get hit. Well, it may be now that that person has gone on to be with the Lord or for some other reason they're now out of the way and I've moved up in rank to the front lines. Well, let me inform you in case you didn't know it, YOU ARE NOW ON THE FRONT LINE. Therefore, God says, "Don't give up."

Galatians 6:7.

> Be not deceived; God is not mocked: for whatsoever a man soweth, that shall he also reap.

Whatever you are reaping now is what you have sown. Don't mock God and say it was God that did it. "God sent me through this to teach me a lesson." Well, if He did, when are you going to learn? We might as well be honest and admit that there are verses in the Bible that we like, and verses that we dislike. We like verses that say, "But my God shall supply all my needs" (Philip. 4:19); but when it comes time for us to do something, we don't like verses that say, "but lay aside every sin and wait" or, "Love thy neighbor as thy self," because those are difficult to obey. There will be somebody that will not like us and, someone that we will not like; however, we must be obedient and not mock God.

Look at (v 8):

> For he that soweth to his flesh shall of the flesh reap corruption;

As a result, if things are destroyed, and subsequently become corrupt and die off, know that you've sown to the flesh. Continuing on (verse 8 and verse 9), read:

> But he that soweth to the Spirit shall of the Spirit reap life everlasting. (v 9) And let us not be weary in well doing: for in due season we shall reap, if we faint not.

Be not weary in well doing or in doing good deeds, for in due season you shall reap **IF** (there's that big word again, only two letters) - if we faint not. If you've ever fainted from a physical stand point you know that sometimes you don't even know that you've fainted! I fainted once and sure enough I didn't even know it. This was years ago; my wife ended up jabbing a knife through her hand trying to separate frozen hamburger patties. I was in taking a shower at the time, trying to be cool - singing, you know, and then suddenly she comes in the bathroom screaming, with blood running everywhere. We get in the car and head to the hospital, and we get there and she's being seen by the doctor. She had her hand closed in a fist, and he began opening her hand up, one finger at a time – and, oh my goodness, when he got to the finger where the wound was, blood squirted up like water from a fountain and I went out like a light; I fainted! I was so outdone.

They had to stop tending to her and tend to me! Later, I'm sitting in a wheelchair asking how it came to be that I was in that chair and they told me what happened and I declared them all to be liars, all of them were lying (of course I was joking – I was just embarrassed). However, the Bible talks about how in the days of adversity if we faint our strength is considered small (Proverbs 24:10). Well, that day my strength was microscopic. Even so, it will happen spiritually to us in those coming days of adversity. Listen, you've quoted this verse:

> (Philip. 4:19) But my God shall supply all your need according to His riches in glory by Christ Jesus.

Afterwards, when harsh conditions really hit, you began to have second thoughts about the Scripture(s) you just quoted, murmuring things like, "He might supply my needs; I think I can do, I don't know. Will He supply my needs?" Thus begins the process: the enemy attempts to further manipulate you into thinking that God cannot supply your needs, and you cannot do whatever God has told you to do, and after a while you'll say, "I don't know why the Lord won't help me." The Devil is reciting - that's right - damnation and doom. You've said it, and now you've sown the seed and you begin to water that seed every day by speaking what you don't desire. You're watching it and now you're cultivating seeds of discord, seeds of negativity, seeds of doubt, and seeds of unbelief, and that's why nothing is happening.

I tried planting grass. I went to the store and rented a roto-tiller, went out and bought the seed; however, I didn't wet the ground first nor did I fertilize or treat the soil. Needless to say, maneuvering the roto-tiller was nothing less than painful for my hands and body. Nonetheless, I planted the seed and I watered it. I got up the next day and looked outside only to see all the birds, with their little heads bobbing up and down, just eating up my seed! After that, blades of grass came up- but in patches. So I tried laying sod instead, but alas, that didn't turn out too well either, it dried up and turned brown.

You have sown one seed of faith within a whole orchard full of negative seeds that have choked the Word, and as a result you're not receiving, but still expecting, a bountiful harvest. You expect to be healed, you expect to be blessed, and you expect to be paid for working – Lord, I thank you right now that all my needs are met. However, you have not done everything you were supposed to do to reap of the one good seed you've sown. Often we look at other people's lives and it looks like they know what they're doing. We look good for a while until we forget to water the sod we've laid down; you looked good for a season. We have to cut out that piece of dried up brown sod, throw it away and replace it with fresh green sod.

What I learned from that whole planting grass experience (I'm speaking spiritually) was that in order to have good, nice, green, and luscious grass you have to first make your ground pliable, keep it watered, and do what needs to be done, spiritually. God wants us to have nice green fertile ground.

The Bible says that He has given you seed; this Bible is nothing but a book of seeds given to you by the Father to take and plant them where they are supposed to be planted. Find new ground and plant more seed, and when you plant more seed and keep making (positive) confessions, eventually you'll till the fallow ground, which is your heart, thus breaking up the wall and hard concreteness of it to receive the Word.

Hebrews 6:12 reads

That ye be not slothful, but followers of them who through faith and patience inherit the promises.

Don't give up; it's going to take faith and patience to inherit; faith and patience. The word "patience" doesn't mean to put up with; it means consistency; faith and continuance. You and I have to continue doing what our minds tell us we're fools to keep doing. We have to continue doing what God wants us to do in spite of what our bodies tell us to do or stop doing even though it looks like I'm not reaping, or it looks like nothings going to happen. The Bible says we have to keep castings our bread out on the water (Eccl. 11:1). Even though the enemy reminds me of worrisome situations, I have to keep casting it out there because if I'm diligent and consistent in that, and if I'm faithful, I will reap.

It is imperative that we understand that when we bend the knee to the enemy we have given the enemy the power, allowing him to plant things inside of us. My thing now is: I will be obedient. As a Teacher of the Gospel I could deliver sermons that make you feel all warm and fuzzy; however, I have to be obedient because if I'm not obedient it's not going to benefit either me or you. God put it on my heart that many of His people have left their first love. You came to God and said "Lord I need a job." He gets you the job. "Lord I need a place." He gets you the place. "Lord I need this, Lord I need that."

You get this or that and although your new place may not be elaborate- no penthouse, but it is fairly nice. No big old super-duper car, but you have means and your need is met and then what happens? We get sucked into these objects and things. We start looking forward to collecting material things allowing them to rule us and we forget that it's God who empowers us to get those things (wealth). We forget who God is, so then the enemy will come in and deceive us even more; he'll try to move us in other ways. For instance, when you sit down to read God's Word. How many times has this happened: when you did make the decision to read the Word, you only read for twenty minutes so you could have time to watch a three hour movie, or maybe you've said, "Okay, I'll go to church- early services," but then later on you think, "Ah, I don't think I'm going to go to service now - I'll go next time." Where are your priorities? What's more important?

We need the Word because the Word brings life, not diversion. If the Word is being delivered through a sermon and it's cutting you to shreds then that's what you need. The Bible says;

(2 Tim. 3:16) All Scripture is given by inspiration of God, and is profitable for doctrine, for **reproof**, for **correction,** for **instruction** in righteousness:

People want to hear things said to them like, "come on up here and let me pray for you." Or, "let me tell you this: the Lord is pleased with you," though a lot of times He is not. We have moved into an area where we need to be amused when we go to church, and if there is no amusement there you won't stay; you'll go where you can be amused and entertained. He's not going to entertain us in heaven, so why do we want to go there? That's a question we must ask ourselves. God is not here to amuse or to entertain us. You don't have to go to church to feel good. If you want amusement and entertainment forget church and forget God.

Faith pleases God, and if we are not operating in faith the Bible says in 1 Corinthians 10:5 that God was not pleased because the children of Israel were overthrown in the wilderness. Now if we're going to please God, we have to stop allowing the "ites" to overthrow us; stop allowing them to get the upper hand. You have an incorruptible crown in sight. What's your incentive? Your incentive to work is called a "pay check." If you go to work and they tell you that you will no longer get paid for the work you do, you would not show up the next day. Well, God has incentives too, not just heaven; He doesn't say "just serve Me" and that's it. There are crowns you can receive; the Crown of Righteousness, the Crown of (soul winners) Rejoicing, the Victors (incorruptible), Crown the Crown of Glory, and the Crown of (withstanding attacks) Life. The Apostle Paul said, "I glory in tribulation;" in essence he's saying, "Come on with it; bring it on."

I would like to share more Scriptures. *God said, "Don't give up,"* and I'm telling you don't have a reason to give up. The Devil is trying to con you-make you think you don't have anything. When he starts telling you, "I'm going to kill you," or "I'm going to take everything away from you," realize that he has shot his last shot. You are already in Canaan and all you have to do is knock him out and you can go on and receive the blessings. However, if you keep backing up into the wilderness, backing up into Egypt, you'll have to start all over again.

Isaiah 55:6 says:

Seek ye the LORD while he may be found call ye upon him while he is near:

Romans 10:8 says:

But what saith it? The word is nigh thee, even in thy mouth, and in thy heart: that is, the word of faith, which we preach.

Now you have to catch this: Isaiah 55:7 says:

Let the wicked forsake his way, and the unrighteous man his thoughts: and let him return unto the LORD, and he will have mercy upon him; and to our God, for he will abundantly pardon. For my thoughts are not your thoughts neither are your ways my ways, saith the LORD (v 8). For as the heavens are higher than the earth, so are my ways higher than yours ways, and my thoughts higher than your thoughts (v 9). For as the rain cometh down, and the snow from heaven and returneth not thither, but watereth the earth, and maketh it bring forth and bud, that it may give seed to the sower, and bread to the eater (v10): So shall my word be that goeth forth out of my mouth: it shall not return unto me void, but it shall accomplish that which I please, and it shall prosper in the thing whereto I sent it.

First, it says, "Seek ye the Lord while He may be found," "call ye upon Him while He is near." You have to speak to Him while He is near. Seek the Lord; Jesus is the Word; the Word is Jesus and the

Word is right here! He is nigh you; the Word is nigh you even in your mouth and in your heart. He is saying, "As My thoughts are higher than your thoughts, as My ways are higher than your ways so is My Word." The Lord showed it to me the one day when it was raining. I was in my car reading and meditating on this Scripture, and He spoke to my spirit saying, "Look around you; see the rain coming down; it does not return to Me in the exact form it left, but as vapor and it's not returning void; it returns only when it does what it needs to do. It prospers everything, it cleans the air, and it waters the grass. The rain doesn't miss anything; it hits everything, and soaks everything; so shall My Word be that comes forth out of *My* mouth; it will not return void."

How does His Word return to Him? It returns when you and I speak it. Listen, God said, "My Word has already covered everything you need in your life, just as the rain and the snow cover everything in their paths." Everything you need is covered by the Word of God. Everything you need is already handled. You're required to be obedient and speak the Word back to Him, so when it returns it will accomplish what it was sent it to do! It's the Word of God. When we speak His Word back to Him, although the "ites", are attacking, it goes back to Him and it doesn't return unto Him void!

You don't have to worry about things and be afraid; all you have to do is "**speak the word**." That's why the Bible says everything that you can see with your eye is temporary. The lack in you life is temporary; sickness is temporary, and disease is temporary. Once upon a time I had an afro; that was temporary. Yeah, I have a little less hair growing up here on my head, but that's all right! At one time, some of us were too able to run the 50-yard dash in record time, but that too was temporary; you may still be able to run it, but not as fast. So what, you have bills; they're temporary; if there is strife that's temporary.

Speak the Word to change it. You know how a thermostat works for a heater: you set the dial at a desired temperature and over a period of time *(as long as everything else is in order)* the home is heated or cooled to the temperature it was set for. So, set the dial on your spiritual thermostat by saying, "I'm the head and not the tail; I'm above and not beneath." *Set it and forget it.* You're going to go through withdrawals because it's cold, but you're only going to shake for a little while; it's temporary. Just say, "No, in Jesus' name, my needs are met; in Jesus' name I can do all things through Christ. In Jesus' name whatever I put my hand to do shall prosper, in Jesus name and you leave it there. You keep saying it: returning the Word to God. Be obedient. That's what we need to do; do it, and God will change everything in your life that needs to be changed.

I don't know about you, but I'm moving in that direction. I have to be obedient because I want His Word, which has already been sent, already covering everything; it's already soaked up everything that I need to have to start working in my life the way He intended it to work in my life. So whatever you're going through, you can go through it with a smile because like Jesus said, "For the joy set before Him..." Jesus was motivated; He went back and endured the cross; He went back and despised the shame of the people because the joy was out there, and the joy was what He was after! I'm after the joy! Glory to God!

Chapter

6

The "Ites"

Coming Face to Face with Them

Exodus 23:28

> And I will send hornets before thee, which shall drive
> out the Hivite, the Canaanite, and the Hittite......

There was something of notable interest in
[v28]. As I was reading, at different times I would
look back at [v23], and I noticed six enemies God
made mention of in this verse. They were the:
Amorites, the Hittites, the Perizzites, the Canaanites,
the Hivites and the Jebusites. That's six, right? Then
I went back over to [v28] and He only mentions three,
the Hivite, the Canaanite, and the Hittite.   So I went
back to my research concerning these "ites" because
the Lord said I needed to know the significance of all
these "ites". I'd ask you to do the same, since God
never mentions things just to be mentioning them, as
if to fill up pages.   Let's turn back and review the
information on pages 27-30, where we discuss the
Amorites, the Hittites, the Perizzites, the Hivites, the
Jebusites, and the Canaanites. So in the preceding
paragraphs you'll get a better understanding of what
you're coming face-to-face with.

The Amorites: These guys will hit you from
above, *the Perizzites* assault you from the outside, *the
Hivites* attack you from the inside, *the Hittites* siege,
cut, and surround you, and *the Canaanites* are the
granddaddy of them all; **their job is to use all the**

other "ites" to get you to bend the knee, so that *the Jebusites* can step on you, keep you under their feet to keep you from emerging. Have you ever tried to hold an animal down? I've played with my dog (in my younger years), and tried to hold him down. They'll squirm and they'll fight to get free from underneath you. It does not matter if it is an animal, or a person, if you are heavy enough, and you keep your weight on them they're unable to go anywhere. The devil tries to do that. Each time you hear a word from God and the heaviness that was on you is lifted off (you've squirmed out a little bit from beneath the enemy's foot) he'll try to hold you down with the other foot, metaphorically speaking. We have to do something to get out from under that dude; use the weapons that God gave you against him.

Now we have all these "ites" that we went over, and referring back to Ex. 23:28 it states: "I will send hornets before thee..." to drive out the Hivites, the people that dwell inward; He's going to drive out the inward junk; He's going to drive out the Canaanite, who will try to humiliate you, bring you to your knees in subjection and He's going to drive out the Hittite, who assails with siege tactics. What was really impressed upon me is that these are the main three that hem us up, and have been successful to a degree. They have been successful until now. Remember when the children of Israel left Egypt headed for Canaan, a land that flowed with milk and honey? Who was there? The enemy, giants of the land, all the "ites;" and in order to take possession of the land they had to fight.

So as it happens, the angel protected Israel and brought them to the "place." You want this land? You want what belongs to you? If the answer is yes then you're going to have to fight for it. **I'll protect you (God says) and I'll guard you but you're going to have to fight.**

Joshua 18:3 states,

And Joshua said unto the children of Israel, How long are ye slack to go to possess the land, which the LORD God of your fathers hath given you?

There were tribes that had already taken possession of the land in different areas of Canaan, and there were some tribes that still hadn't claimed their inheritance. He (Joshua) asked how long they were going to wait, why they were taking so long to possess what's theirs. Which tribe are you? *See, basically He was asking why are you still in this position?* How many of us are still wandering in the wilderness when everybody else is already in Canaan?

There used to be a song that my aunts and cousins sang all the time, and I believe that the title of the song was "Standing Here Wondering Which Way to Go". Now please, do not get upset with me for this statement. I am by no means making fun nor belittling anyone; I understood what they were saying, however, we don't need to be standing around wondering which way to go. We need to know which way we're going. If the angel is sent before you to take you to the place (which is face-to-face with the "Ites"), then there is no question of which way to go. What we're going to do is run all the "ites" out, and any grand-kids that they may have out in order to possess the land! God says, "I will not drive them out before the year." Now don't misread this and think that God wants you to suffer a little while longer; that's not the case. You and I have to learn how to take possession of the land properly.

Let's say we'd like to win a city and bring about reform. We need a new Mayor, new board members, a new this and a new that, and we'd like them all to be Christians. If we as Christians don't know (from the Word of God) how a city should be run, and how to appeal to the masses- honey, the city may be in worse condition than what it was. Some may say, "Nah, it cannot be, because God would be in control," but if the Christian – saved, sanctified, and filled with the Holy Ghost, but just as messed up as you want to be - doesn't know first of all how to hear God's voice and obey God as well as being skilled in their appointed duties, then the mistake would be that we're now torn between two things. You'd go in there as a Christian with Christian values, trying to run a city that bases everything on carnal values. "If I do it this way then......uh, this is not going to work, If I do it this way...... I don't exactly know how to do it the way God wants me to do it." You need to learn how to skillfully do what needs to be done.

So, God says, "I want you to get to a point where you're not that way." And little by little, as you gain ground and you learn who you are, you can take some authority and then as you gain more ground, take more authority, gain even more ground, take even more authority, so on and so forth. Then the next thing you know you're not down there in the valley anymore, you're up on the mountain top! God is the only one who knows how things should be done. When you really stop and think about it, God *is* smarter than we are. He's not going to immediately place you or me in positions we aren't ready for.

For instance, how should we operate God's finances? Plant a seed and leave it planted, do not dig it up; sow seeds. The world's method is to dig it up, get as much as you can and keep it for yourself. The world's motto is, "Believe it when you see it". But God's is "Believe it before you see it!" How can you say you're going to take authority over the city and do all these things? How are you going to accomplish these things when you (personally) have trouble believing God for $50.00? A city needs millions.

The Lord has been trying to show me this for a while and I started getting into it at one point, and then things would come up and distract me. Nevertheless, I was finally able to get *this out* and get what God was saying to me because, it shows the pattern; it shows where He actually takes us after we pray about something, and the process of it all. Some may think, well now Brother Pastor, just wait a minute; God doesn't lead us into temptation; He doesn't send us through tests and trials; and it's true, He doesn't. Nonetheless, in order for the children of Israel to possess Canaan they had to go through the wilderness. There was no other way around it. And now that we are in the Land......... see, we are in the "land" right now, spiritually and physically (but really more spiritually) that flows with milk and honey. We have to overcome things, so God has to bring you to that place to conquer your enemy; to deal with what needs to be dealt with. God's not trying to tempt you; He's not trying to test you; He's not teaching you a lesson, and He's not trying to do anything of the kind. That is not of God, for God already knows what you're going to do; however, you're the one who prayed! You're the one that said, "I believe, God;" so He said, "Okay, I'll send My angel before you;" and He sent His angel before us to lead us in the way. Look at Isaiah 48:17

> Thus saith the LORD, thy Redeemer, the Holy One of Israel; I am the LORD thy God, which teacheth thee to profit, which leadeth thee by the way that thou shouldest go.

Now, most of the time when the Bible talks about the *Angel of the Lord* in the Old Testament, it's talking about Jesus. He went before them to lead them to the place. See, Jesus said He would teach us to profit and He would lead us in the way that we should go. He didn't say he would make you rich by dumping all the money on you along with everything else and just leave you, but He said He's going to take us to a place and then we have to do the rest. When we do what God says: come out against the enemy, and then He'll be an enemy to our enemies. Its not, "Lord this is what's happened," and then God says, "Okay, now I see what happened, I'm glad you woke me up." You know that is not God's character because after it's all said and done, and you've prayed and said, "I'm standing on Your Word and I am doing this," the Lord says, "Okay, I see that; I see you standing on the Word; now I'm going to bring you to that thing – face-to-face." And if it's in you it's going to surface. Don't suppress it or be in denial about it, or it will never come out and you'll not get the victory.

Some people have bad attitudes and God wants to bring it out; sometimes it comes up during confrontations with others. Ask me how I know that one! It's happened to me and I'm telling you I could not figure it out. I thought what in the world is going on here? I will never forget the time some Ministers came to my home years ago; they weren't even trying to live the way that God expected *(as far as I knew)*, but had the nerve to come to my house after I'd preached a message, and said, "You shouldn't have said 'you' in your message; you should have said 'we';" and then started saying some other things, and I'm sitting there at the end of the table fuming, angry. Can you empathize with me on that one? I'm sitting there thinking how dare these people come in my house and try to tell me how to minister.....and they aren't doing anything for God *(again, as far as I knew)*. Oh no! (I said within myself – I was about to go off). But you know what the Lord told me? He said, "Shut up and listen." Shut up and listen! I couldn't understand why. Now this is a big problem for a lot of folks.

I had that problem. I didn't want to listen, and I didn't want to hear what anybody had to say. I'm right. I know I'm right. I didn't care what they thought. God called me to preach; don't tell me anything. I know it happens and at that very moment He was teaching me this very thing, but I didn't know it then. I didn't know it. God was showing me that when things come up it's because it has to be dealt with by *you*. That's why I say all the time, work on you, not someone else. WORK ON YOURSELF. Not those guys *(other people around you)*, these guys, you know- Me, myself, and I. Deal with them and God will help you.

Let the other person have the problem; just make sure you don't have it. You walk in love; they'll catch on and if they don't, you better make sure you catch it. It's always you. You get yourself together. You come up; let the angel bring you to the "place." He will protect you, and that protection remains even while you're in the "place". Do what you have to do; handle your business. Step on the Devil; deal with those highlanders and deal with all of them because you have the authority. Then you will come out with a smile on your face.

The enemy wants your head to hang low, but the Word says, "He is the lifter up of my head."

(Ps 3:3) But thou, O LORD, art a shield for me; my glory, and the lifter up of mine head.

So if you look sad all the time, something is wrong and what does it say about your relationship with God? Is there is no peace, no joy, and no victory? It has to be some kind of victory someplace. Praise the Lord! God is a good God! When you stop and think about what God has done, and about His goodness, all you should be able to do is worship and praise the Lord!

Chapter
7

Understanding the Process

Revelation Knowledge is Key

Now, I would like for you to go back with me to Exodus 23. God really spoke to us out of this passage of Scripture, and He is still speaking. Exodus chapter 23:20-23.

> Behold, I send an Angel before thee, to keep thee in the way, and to bring thee into the place which I have prepared (v20). Beware of him, and obey his voice, provoke him not; for he will not pardon your transgressions: for my name is in him (v21). But thou shall indeed obey his voice, and do all that I speak; then I will be an enemy unto thine enemies, and an adversary unto thine adversaries (v22). For mine Angel shall go before thee, to bring thee in unto the Amorites, and the Hittites, and the Perizzites, and the Canaanites, the Hivites, and the Jebusites (v23): [the Devilites and the Demonites- I've added those] and I will cut them off.

Let's pause right here. We know, according to Scripture, God said that He sent the angel before. You and I have a personal angel and the Bible speaks about it in the Book of Matthew,

> (Matt. 18:10) Take heed that ye despise not one of these little ones; for I say unto you, That in heaven their angels do always behold the face of my Father which is in heaven.

It reminds us that we need to watch how we treat children because their angels are always before the throne of God.

Just because you are older now doesn't mean that you've out grown the angel you had as a child.

Your personal angel is no wimp, and angels are not cupids. They're not these little fat babies with bows and arrows, and if you study the Word you'll find that angels are a minimum 12 to 13 plus feet tall. Can you imagine Goliath and his brothers being that tall? Can you imagine standing there talking about, "I'm going to whoop you?" Saul's amour, the coat of mail, which Saul wanted David to wear weighed almost 200 pounds (1 Sam. 17:38). Now, how would you deal with Goliath and that? Have you ever tried to lift 200 pounds? You may be able to hold it for a few seconds but that's all! But here we're dealing with Angelic Hosts that are strong and mighty; they're not "almighty," but they're strong in might.

The angel is there to keep you. The word "keep" means *to guard and to protect.* Not just when you were a little baby, but after you've gotten old; sometimes ignorant and sometimes foolish, but somebody's prayers delivered you. We are walking along this path and there are obstacles that get us off track. There are things that will come and cause you to make a right turn or a left turn when you are not supposed to turn at all; you were supposed to keep straight. There may come a time when God will have us turn, but only at His discretion. Sometimes we're impatient with God and we'll attempt to tackle the problem on our own because we think we're ready, and we can handle it. You know, every now and then we think we're all that! Perhaps you know and can quote some Scriptures; have a couple of Bibles and a dictionary at the house, and you're ready to part Red Seas. Now it may be that the Word of God isn't developed enough in you to part that Red Sea. Yet in denial, we run out with zeal and no knowledge and no anointing, saying, "I can do all things through Christ." Yes you can, except the Word of God is not permeated in you. As stated in the book of Acts, Faith in the name of Jesus is what's needed:

(Acts 3:16) And His name, through **faith in His name,** hath made this man strong, whom ye see and know: yea, the faith which is by him hath given him this perfect soundness in the presence of you all.

Too many times we use the Name of Jesus, but our Faith in that Name is weak. Listen to this: from time to time our confessions are made out of fear and desperation, and not in faith. You're afraid you're going to lose or not get whatever, and you say, "I better make this confession." Just think about it - if you're afraid, there's no faith in it. Its like: I'd better hurry up and do this because I'm supposed to. For example, when we give of our tithes and offering, we give because we know we're supposed to, but are we giving in faith? So many times there is no return because we haven't given in faith. We made an offer unto God, with our offerings, yet He refuses it. Were we giving because we're supposed too? Everything must be done in faith if we're going to receive from God; this is the way it has to be done. We say things sometimes in despair and God will hear us sometimes in that despair, but because of intercessory prayer (others praying for you) blessings still come through; but if you keep coming to God in despair, and keep making your confessions based on fear, then your tithes and your offerings are given in vain. So I have to get to a point where I'm not coming to Him in fear or dread that I'm going to lose this or that. Heb. 11:6 says:

But without faith it is impossible to please Him: **for he that cometh to God must believe that He is**, and that He is a rewarder of them that diligently seek Him.

Let's say, for example, that God has put it on your heart to pray for me, and you just don't feel like praying, and now I'm left holding the bag; I'm in a state of despair and nothing is happening. Let me say this, there are times we'll go to God and we'll say we are in need of this, that, or the other and the need is urgent. The Bible says, "He that believeth shall not make haste." Why? Because: You know the outcome. Therefore, if you really believe, then time is of no matter because in God there is no time. God is always, when? Not on time; but He's always now. In order to receive from God we have to move from the past, and we have to move from the future to **NOW**. When are you healed? Now! When are you blessed? Now!

All you needs are met when? Now! But if you look at your checking account and it says, "No, they aren't! Your needs are not met," but to God it is. Subsequently, when you pray *(which is now)* and then tomorrow comes, your thanksgiving should be in the now. In other words, I thank you Father today because I prayed yesterday and I thank you Father now, for what I prayed about yesterday.

Because if I say, "Father, again I come to you on behalf of what I prayed about yesterday." Then pray that same day what you prayed about yesterday. You're not in the "now". And because you didn't believe it when you prayed you didn't receive it. The Bible says, "When you pray believe you receive." So when, would when you pray be? If you pray now, you have to believe you've received it at that moment and if you believe you've received it at that moment then tomorrow thank God for what you prayed about the day before or yesterday!

If the manifestation of what you prayed for tarries, then next week thank God for what you prayed about last week. And if it continues to tarry, then next year thank God for what you prayed about last year! It's keeping the prayer in the "now." We have to abide by and live by time. **God has no time**. Now, I'm going to say something that you might disagree with. I won't judge you if you've made this kind of statement because I've made the same statement myself. I'm just trying to make a point. We say and have been saying, *"It's all going to work out in God's time."* How many times have you heard someone say that? There's really nothing wrong with this statement. I believe in timing – that is, I believe that at certain times there are windows of opportunity for you and me. And we need to take advantage of the opportunity at that time – but, again God doesn't set the course for you or me. James 3:6 says,

> And the tongue is a fire, a world of iniquity: so is the tongue among our members, that it defileth the whole body, and setteth on fire the course of nature; and it is set on fire of hell.

It is the tongue that sets the very course of your life, not God. Therefore you, by your words establish your own window of opportunity for your life. You see, this planet is set on a course dictated by time. There is a time for everything; a time for seasons to change, and a time for animals to migrant and hibernate. See, things operate and function on this planet because God set it in motion by His Word. And because God is omniscient (having infinite awareness, understanding and insight) different events happen to prophetically fulfill His Word. Often we think this means that calamity is a season of tribulation we go through, set into motion by God. And when He thinks you've had enough you'll come out. God has nothing to do with your situation. I want you to think about it. He said He sent His angel before you to keep you; however, the angel is not going to keep you if you don't want to be kept. You know, God has a purpose in all He does. All He's going to do is prepare a path so that we'll have a way to go and He'll lead us in the "way" and we must follow. If we choose not to follow, the angel isn't going to make you go the way that God has planned for you. **WE HAVE TO BE WILLING TO GO. WE HAVE TO FOLLOW. WE HAVE TO WALK.**

Often in our prayers, or should I say in our expectation of how God should operate in our lives; we assume that He is going to grab us and force us to go in a certain direction but He's not. The Bible tells us too obey the voice of the angel, or any agent that God sends to assist us in whatever it is we need assistance with. Whether it's the Holy Ghost, or whether it's Jesus, or whether it's His angels. We need to heed their voices and obey. God can send all the angels He wants to. He can prepare the pathway. He can do all these things, but if we don't obey; we have a problem.

When we find out that He is bringing us to place and that place is not La-de-da Land. It is not, "I'm care free I don't have to do anything land." But it's a place we don't expect Him to take us; to our enemy. He says it right here (Ex. 23:22) "... bring thee in unto the Amorites, the Hitities, the Hivities, the Canaanites, the Perzzites, the Jebusites...," and all the other "ites." And there is one I didn't even mention Girgasite. All the "ites" are problems, unsettling situations, things that hinder you to keep you from receiving what is in Canaan.

The children of Israel, and all that they experienced was a model of the church. Egypt was a model of the world. Pharaoh was a model of Satan. Moses was a model of Christ. The Bible says that we should read and study what they did in the Old Testament because they're actions are examples for us (1Cor. 10:11). God was leading them out of some conditions, but they had to be obedient in order to get out of Egypt (Ex.12). There the putting of blood on the lintel of the doors; there was a specific way the lamb had to be roasted; and bitter herb and unleavened bread had be to eaten with it; and certain things they had to say; and once they did that, then

God delivered them out of Egypt with a mighty hand. Moreover, when He delivered them out of Egypt He brought them to a "place," but they had to go through the wilderness to get to that place.

The wilderness is a type of your flesh and your flesh, *I would say,* is probably more of an enemy to you than the Devil. Your flesh, together with your mind, your will, and your emotions (that make up the soul), and all the other inward parts of the belly can be a tremendous hindrance. We can mess up; we can get in the way of whatever God is trying to do. God could give you a message for somebody, just maybe a couple of words and that's all you'll need to say, but for some reason, when it leaves the lips of God or one of His agents to us, we have a tendency of taking what's pure and perfect and messing it up. We inject some of "us" in it...... thinking maybe we need to add a little more to make it really believable. So here we go, "Thus saith the Lord thy God," and you run on about all kinds of stuff. Yet you know God didn't tell you to say all that. Nothing's wrong with saying, "Thus saith the Lord thy God," but what I'm saying is that the majority of the time we add what we think God would say.

A keyboard, for all practical purposes is perfect. Now, when a person who is not familiar with playing a keyboard makes an attempt too play, you will not hear good sounds. Isn't that right? But when a person who has learned through experience and practice sits down- sweet melodies are heard. See now, the same thing is true spiritually.

You and me, we have a lot of work to do. We are imperfect vessels that have been given a perfect gift. We have to learn how to minister; we have to learn how to talk, walk, act, hear, and obey God's Word. The Word of God is pure; the Word is perfect in itself; there are no flaws.

Now I want to dig into [v 24] a little bit more too bring to your attention some of the Hebrew words mentioned here. The first word we are going to look at is the word "not", in [v 24] "Thou shall not....." the second word is "nor" and the two words together "bow down" The third is the word "overthrow," the word "images," and then the word "breakdown;" this is so we can get a clear understanding of what God is saying.

The word "not" means never. The words "not" and "nor" both mean never. In Hebrew, the word has the same meaning. The two words "bow" and "down" together mean to lie prostrate, especially in homage, as to God; to crouch, to worship. The word "serve" means to labor, to work, to worship. The meaning of the word "overthrow" really moved me since I've never seen it expressed like this before; it means to pull down in pieces; to break, to destroy, to beat down, pluck down, pull down, throw down and *"destroy utterly."* The word "images" is in reference to an image of an idol. And last but not least "break down" means to crush, to destroy, to tear or hurt. I'm going to put all these words and their meaning together and we'll see how this verse may be interpreted. The 24th verse could read as follows:

> Thou shall never lie prostrate or crouch, especially in homage, as to God, or worship other gods; never labor, work or worship them, never do after their works: but thou shall utterly destroy, beat down, pluck down, pull down, and throw them down in pieces, and "ex" them utterly out; and quite break them down .....

Did you know you can hurt those demons? You know you've wanted to hurt them, to hurt their idols, and their imaginations (empty fanciful notions). This really stirred me. I was sitting there and I said "imagination," and the Lord spoke and said in Matthew 12:36 and 37:

> But I say unto you that every idol word that men shall speak they shall give account thereof in the day of judgment by thy words thou shall be justified and by thy words thou shall be condemned.

I remember preaching a message on the image of God titled "In His Image." It brought to mind that we are created in His image; God imagined us. He didn't just wake up one morning and say, "I'm going to make a man." He meditated on what we were to be and then one day He spoke us into existence. We are products of the spoken word. You have to catch this. We are products of what was spoken by God after He formed man from the dust of the ground. He breathed the breath of life (Himself) into man, and man became a living soul. Jesus said in (John. 6:63), "....the words that I speak unto you, they are spirit, and they are life." So every word you speak is spirit, and it can be either spirit and life or spirit and death. Jesus didn't say, "My words are spirit and death" because there is no death in Him (John 1:4). That's why He said in (Matt. 12:37), by our words we will be justified and by our words we will be condemned, because we're in a position of choice.

We choose our words, and the words you speak on continual basis create images. We now know that images are statues or mental pictures of something that was produced by a figure of speech, especially metaphors, and so these are things that God said He was going to bring us face-to-face with in (v 24) so that we can hurt, break, and pull down those images, not bow down to them. He's bringing us to a place. Often we're the problem; it isn't the Devil all the time; it's those little statues we've created of low self esteem, depression, poverty, addiction, and what others say about us. You need to get a hammer or mallet and break up those little images. The Word says you are somebody in Christ; you are a new creature in Christ; "a new creation." You are not that image you were before. Praise the Lord! We've all gone through something or another and we get in the presence of God and we repent, and God speaks to us and we get back on the prepared path.

Before, we were over there running into all kinds of obstacles; people can be obstacles. But if we get ourselves on the path, and pray before God, the angel will lead us in the way; we're being obedient, and that's the way it should be. Yet when we move in that direction, there may be a wall there and that wall will consist of those little statues, the images, the Amorites, the Canaanites, all the other "ites", which we've created or allowed others to create in us. Now, if you don't watch it you'll start complaining; you'll start backing up, wanting to go back to Egypt, thinking as the children of Israel thought; as they said, "At least we had three squares over there in Egypt."

If you remember they complained and complained! First they want to be delivered. Then when they were delivered, they recanted when they ran into the "wall", and said, "We had it better in Egypt". Well, what do you want? So we must look at our condition and see where we are. God has brought us to our enemies; to those idols, and it's our job to destroy them. Don't try to get them all at once; take your time; all you have is time, and just deal with one dude at a time.

When I was a kid, my dad gave me a little work shop set; you know with a saw that didn't cut very well, and the little screw driver, and a hammer about 6" to 7" long similar to a ball-peen hammer like the one the guy used to break out of prison with in the movie "The Shawshank Redemption" (if you recall). You may start out with a little hammer; nonetheless, it's a hammer and it represents the Word of God. I don't care if you have to start chipping away at the little toes on the idol, just do something and the next thing you know, that joker will become rubble and dust…. You've seen how they demolish old buildings with that big old wrecking ball? Next thing you know, your hammer has turned into one of those and you can just start swinging way; you have time. God told you to break it up. Break it up! Don't just cut the legs off and leave it there and move on, because if you come back you'll still recognize it. God wants it destroyed, not just cut down a bit. "Oh, praise the Lord I've cut them down," and then you go back and evoke it. The "Ites" are not destroyed; you have to kill them and cut them down so they're not standing up or lying down chatting with you any more. Destroy them, cut them up, and "ex" them utterly out! I don't know, and I cannot recollect how many times I thought about things I thought I would never think about again, and then I reflected upon why it came back. The Devil is out there trying to work his way in; but a lot of times it isn't the Devil, it's **us -** because we have not destroyed it. Instead, we've suppressed it. Then it comes back; resurrected……, "Night of the Living Idols," or whatever you want to call it, walking around at night trying to reunite with you again. You assumed that you got rid of them. They're all outside,…you've seen the movies; so you know what I'm talking about. They're all outside hanging on the windows and you know what we'll do? We do just as they do in the movies, we run from them. No, we need to kill them! Get rid of them.

I trust that you are able to identify with what I'm saying here because just as the children of Israel saw the disasters that lay ahead, you can see disaster as well.

Consequently, the words you speak create the images that create the idols. So I have a question.

What have you been saying? Have you been using the Word of God to speak against that affliction and hardship? When you use the Word of God like a hammer, and strike out repeatedly on the walls of burden, strife, and fear. It's going to tear it down. If you start saying the opposite of what the Word says, you are adding more problems to your life. You are reinforcing the wall, so when you do come to God with a little prayer it isn't going to achieve anything. You have this huge statue that you've put all kinds of rebar and concrete into; pile driven it down in the ground; and here you come with a little hammer (your prayer).

That hammer (prayer) is going to bounce off and you'll cry out and say, "I want this down." We've built the thing so strong that now we have to stand in there and deal with it. Just keep saying everyday, "Father I thank you right now that I'm redeemed; I thank you that I'm free; I thank you Father that I'm delivered; thank you Father in Jesus' name." We have to stay with it everyday; in thanksgiving, everyday! It will transform the little itty-bitty things into something meaningful. It's God's way of telling us that all of this pertains to obedience.

Now listen, Canaan has never been, and is not a type of Heaven. You know why? Because the enemy is in Canaan; there are no enemies in Heaven. Will you agree with me on that? Can you imagine doing all this fighting and suffering, and then when we finally make it into heaven, we have to fight some more? I don't think so! You might as well stay with the devil; just go on and go to hell and be done with it! But thank God that isn't the case. As I stated earlier, God said to me, **"You're fighting them because they have your inheritance; they got your stuff"**. They have your healing. They have your deliverance. They have your money. They have your peace. They have everything you're supposed to have. Canaan *(in the Bible)* was a land flowing with milk and honey; everything they needed was there in abundance. Can you imagine a cluster of grapes so immense two guys had to carry it? Can you imagine a grape so big that three to four people could eat of it? Can you imagine that? That's how Canaan was. For all intended purposes, Canaan is a type of the Baptism of the Holy Ghost, and walking in our rights and privileges in God, walking in victory. Our Canaan is what I've been talking about. That's our Canaan land.

"Every place (Josh. 1:3) that the soles of your foot shall tread upon, that have I given you....." Why is it that I haven't had what I should've had? Maybe it's because the soles of my feet haven't trod there yet. I remember as a young Baptist boy, I didn't know nor understand anything about the Baptism of the Holy Ghost. Why? The soles of my feet had never trodden upon those Scriptures that spoke of it. So we need to get our shoes on and get to stepping, because there are some areas we need to have in our lives that those "ites" have, and they shouldn't have it. God gave it to you, so go get you stuff! That's what you have to do, go get it! Don't constantly remind the Lord of your needs. He knows your needs, but He has already supplied them for you! He said, "Here's Canaan; here it is, it's yours." Now, when you get the title deed to your home you say, "Praise God. It's mine; thank you for my home."

We need to go get what's ours. But we're not going to get it without a fight; so don't go in the ring as if you are trying to win a title. You're defending your title. You're not trying to be the champ, **YOU ARE THE CHAMP;** and the Holy Spirit is your coach. He's telling you to put your guard up; don't try to go in there and dance around and do all this fancy stuff, because you'll get splattered. You'll come back with your eye all swollen; and now you need prayer, now you need to be healed. You've already been in there and you know what to do, so do what you've done in practice. Don't try to change your style in the ring and trip over your feet. Many times the Holy Spirit has picked you up because you couldn't get up. So don't go into the ring like you're nobody; you are somebody!

First, start chipping away at those idols, all the things that you have been saying that was contrary to God's Word. Some of you may have a lighted glass curio with all your figurines inside. Well, spiritually speaking, all those idols you have standing up in a glass curio, they have got to go. Get those jokers out; they've been around so long they've become old acquaintances; even to the point to where you say, "my arthritis; my headache; my this; my that; my kidney stones". Well, they'll give them, to you in a jar if you request them but don't show them to me. I don't want to see anything relative to your kidney stones; it isn't yours. They aren't mine and they're not yours. Deal with all the "ites", even if you have to write them down or sit them down in your bedroom or your living room or wherever it is. Give each one of them a chair; call a meeting and stand there and say, "I'm really glad you came to this meeting. "The meeting shall now come to order; all you jokers are fired. You're fired because you've been trying to siege me; you're fired, et cetera." Whatever you have to do; however the Holy Spirit moves you. Get rid of them.

If we can just understand the process, that is understand that after we've prayed, (brace yourself) we have just caused that which was in us to surface; then comes test and trial that God didn't send - and this trial is an "Ite," and the "Ite" could be anything. You want deliverance in manifestation, that's why you cried out to God. God says, "OK, you want to be free; Angel, take him face-to-face with the 'Ites' [your sin or problem], so that he may utterly destroy them.

Do not bow down by yielding to them again. God has already made a way of escape for us. Once we see this, we'll be like Paul and our fight will be a good fight. What is a good fight? One that you know you've already won!

A Prayer for the Reader

I just sense that we need to pray for one another. Some of the idols in our lives are very, very strong and you may need help; we need help from time to time from others in prayer. This, of course, doesn't mean that you cannot tackle it yourself, because you've been chipping away; but some of those jokers need to be blown up; we need some dynamite. So that's why we *need* and have each other. Allow me to pray this prayer with you.

Father, today thank You; I thank You right now Father for Your wisdom, knowledge, revelation, and understanding as to what to do to come out against these "ites", to come out against them and destroy them. To overcome them, overthrow them, to get them out of our lives; to get rid of all imagination, to get rid of all imagery and idolatry in the name of Jesus. I thank You Father right now for it. I praise you Father right now in the name of Jesus Christ. In Jesus name, I come against every evil spirit; I come against every wrong thought, in the name of Jesus Christ, and I come against anything and everything that is opposed to the Word of God, in the name of Jesus Christ.

And I thank you Father right now for your anointing that shall destroy! That shall break every yoke! In the name of Jesus, I speak it into their lives. I speak it into all of our lives, and it is so because you said it to be so in Your Word, and we are speaking Your Word. Not what we think, not what we feel but what you said, and we thank you Father that it is done in our lives. It is done in our personal lives, it is done in our homes, it is done on our jobs, it is done in this ministry, and it is done, Father, in other ministries. It is done for the Body of Christ! In Jesus name, thank you Father right now. Thank You Lord. And peradventure Father, if there is anyone that is not saved, if there is anyone that is not a Christian, I thank You right now that they should receive; cry out to the Lord! And that they shall receive Jesus Christ as their Lord and Savior. Come into their lives Father and make them new creatures. I thank you Lord right now for their anointing to heal and to deliver and to be set free. I give You the praise; I give You the glory in Jesus name, Amen.

In His Service,
Pastor Alvin L. Armstrong

www.ingramcontent.com/pod-product-compliance
Lightning Source LLC
Chambersburg PA
CBHW060421050426
42449CB00009B/2060